MW01102105

ABORIGINAL TREATIES

BY CAROLYN GRAY

Weigl

Published by Weigl Educational Publishers Limited
6325 10th Street SE
Calgary, Alberta, Canada T2H 2Z9
Website: www.weigl.com

Library and Archives Canada Cataloguing in Publication data available upon request.
Fax (403) 233-7769 for the attention of the Publishing Records department.

ISBN 978-1-55388-692-1 (hard cover)
ISBN 978-1-55388-697-6 (soft cover)

Printed in the United States of America in North Mankato, Minnesota
1 2 3 4 5 6 7 8 9 0 14 13 12 11 10

072010
WEP230610

All of the Internet URLs given in the book were valid at the time of publication. However, due to the dynamic nature of the Internet, some addresses may have changed, or sites may have ceased to exist since publication. While the author and publisher regret any inconvenience this may cause readers, no responsibility for any such changes can be accepted by either the author or the publisher.

Weigl acknowledges Getty Images as its primary image supplier for this title.

Every reasonable effort has been made to trace ownership and to obtain permission to reprint copyright material. The publishers would be pleased to have any errors or omissions brought to their attention so that they may be corrected in subsequent printings.

We acknowledge the financial support of the Government of Canada through the Canada Book Fund for our publishing activities.

EDITORS: Josh Skapin and Aaron Carr
DESIGN: Terry Paulhus

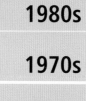

Aboriginal Treaties
Through The Years

European explorers first arrived in North America in 1492 and found the continent populated by Aboriginal Peoples. The land was rich in resources, including water, wood, minerals, and furs. The first European settlers made pacts with Aboriginal Peoples. These pacts included the right to hunt, trade, and live on Aboriginal lands. In exchange, European settlers traded manufactured goods with Aboriginal Peoples. Some of the goods included iron, tools, and weapons. Aboriginal Peoples soon became known among the settlers for their hunting skill and knowledge. This led to the fur trade, in which Aboriginal Peoples traded animals pelts for goods.

In addition to making pacts with Europeans, Aboriginal Peoples made political agreements among themselves. Most of these early treaties were oral in nature. Some were recorded on wampum belts. These belts were woven with thousands of coloured shells and were designed to illustrate events. Aboriginal Peoples felt trade and friendship were connected. They would befriend people who were able to help them.

As Aboriginal Peoples thought of trade and friendship as the same, they would "adopt" people with whom it was helpful to be on good terms. Aboriginal Peoples brought European settlers into their families through rituals and ceremonies. These first treaty relationships formed the basis of Canada.

Over time, the relationship between European settlers and Aboriginal Peoples changed significantly. Customs changed as settlers began to establish their place on the continent. Traditional Aboriginal ways of life started to be replaced by European practices. Oral pacts and wampum belts were replaced with written treaties. Ceremony and friendship were no longer the basis of Aboriginal and settler relations. Aboriginal Peoples were subjected to laws passed by the settlers. The main basis of these laws was the **Indian Act** of 1876. The laws in this act were designed to conform Aboriginal Peoples to the cultures of the settlers. Treaties required Aboriginal Peoples to give up the rights to their land. In return, they were promised **reserves**, education, hunting and fishing rights, and cash payments.

Aboriginal Treaties
2000s

The Peace of the Braves

2002

The Peace of the Braves

The Peace of the Braves, or the Agreement Respecting a New Relationship Between the Cree Nation and the Government of Quebec, is a treaty between the Government of Quebec, the Government of Canada, and the Grand Council of Crees. The treaty was signed in February 2002. The title of the agreement is a reference to a 1701 peace treaty between the French and **Iroquois League**. The agreement honours the obligations the Quebec government made to the Cree people in the 1975 James Bay Agreement. The treaty grants joint legal power over the James Bay area to both the Cree and the provincial government. In exchange, the Cree agreed to allow the Quebec government to develop hydroelectric facilities in the area. The Peace of the Braves is notable as one of the first treaties that did not require the **First Nation** involved to give up its territory claims in order to pursue a settlement.

2001

British Columbia Premier Gordon Campbell calls for a referendum on Aboriginal treaty principles.

2002

British Columbia holds a referendum on treaty negotiations.

2003

The federal government approves giving financial compensation to former students of residential schools.

Lieutenant's Book Program

Model National Policy

2004

Lieutenant Governor's Book Program

James Bartleman, a member of the Chippewas of Mnjikaning First Nation, was the 27th lieutenant governor of Ontario from 2002 to 2007. Included in his term was a commitment to improve the inadequate education opportunities for Aboriginal youth. He began the Lieutenant Governor's Book Program to promote literacy development for First Nations, **Métis**, and **Inuit** youth.

2009

Model National Policy

In 2009, the Land Claims Agreements Coalition (LCAC) released a model national policy that outlined how land claims agreement should be implemented. The LCAC is a government-funded organization that works to ensure comprehensive land claims and self-government agreements are respected. The LCAC stated that promises of modern treaties remain unfulfilled. Paul Kaludjak, co-chair of the coalition and president of Nunavut Tunngavik Inc. said the intention of the model policy is to start a national discussion about ongoing federal-Aboriginal relations, specifically with regard to treaties. In a prepared statement, the LCAC said it believes a new national policy is needed to ensure that all modern treaties are fully implemented. The federal **Crown** has been involved in 21 modern treaties with Aboriginal Peoples across Canada since 1975. These agreements involve more than half of the country's lands, waters, and resources. The treaties are recognized and affirmed by the Constitution of Canada.

2004

The Canada-Aboriginal Peoples Roundtable is held in Ottawa to discuss the future direction of First Nations communities.

2005

The federal government establishes a $1.9-billion compensation package for the students of residential schools.

2005

Kelowna Accord

The Kelowna Accord promised immediate action to improve the quality of life for Canadian Aboriginals in the areas of health, education, housing, and relationships. The accord, which was signed in November 2005, was based on a series of agreements between the Government of Canada, the provincial premiers, and national Aboriginal leaders. This discussion took 18 months to complete. The positive process of co-operation and group deliberation was halted when the Liberal government lost a vote of **non-confidence** in Parliament. The Conservative Party formed the government. However, the Conservative government has yet to implement the agreement.

2008

Aboriginal Schools

On June 11, 2008, Prime Minister Stephen Harper apologized to former students of residential schools. "The treatment of children in Indian residential schools is a sad chapter in our history," Harper said. "Today, we recognize that this policy of assimilation was wrong, has caused great harm, and has no place in our country." This apology was related to 19th century treaties. Two of these early treaties were the Act for the Protection of the Indians in Upper Canada and the Act to Encourage the Gradual Civilization of Indian Tribes. The apology also related to amending laws related to Aboriginal Peoples, also known as the Gradual Civilization Act. These acts made attendance at residential schools mandatory for Aboriginal children. The schools were intended to force assimilation, or to absorb Aboriginal children completely into European ways of life.

Kelowna Accord

2006

A $2 billion compensation settlement for Canadian Aboriginals forced to attend residential schools is effectively settled in Canadian courts on December 15.

2007

Steven Point is named British Columbia's first Aboriginal lieutenant governor.

Into the Future

Saskatchewan schools were the first in Canada to teach students about Aboriginal treaties as a mandatory part of their curriculum. "This is a good step toward using education to eliminate some of the misconceptions of Treaty," Federation of Saskatchewan Indian Nations Vice-Chief Lyle Whitefish said. "We are all Treaty people and that includes non-First Nation citizens. We all have a responsibility to learn more and understand the Treaty relationship." What did Chief Lyle Whitefish mean when he said, "We are all Treaty People"?

2008

The Senate standing committee on Aboriginal Peoples reports that federal practices and policy on modern treaties decreases benefits to Aboriginal Peoples.

2009

The first modern treaty negotiated under the British Columbia Treaty Commission process takes effect.

Aboriginal Treaties
1990s

1990

The Oka Crisis

In Oka, Quebec, the local government planned to build a golf course on a sacred burial ground of the Mohawk nation. The plan resulted in tension between the two sides. On July 11, 1990, several Mohawks of the Kanesatake reserve set up a barricade to prevent construction of the golf course. Quebec provincial police in riot gear attempted to break through the barricade and end the blockade. The attempt resulted in a 15-minute confrontation that included tear gas and gunshots fired on both sides. The police retreated, but 31-year-old officer Marcel Lemay was shot and killed during the incident. For the most part, the violence ended on the first day, but the resistance lasted another 77 days before coming to an end. As tensions rose, the Canadian Armed Forces were called in to oversee the situation. On September 26, after attempts at negotiation failed, the Mohawks put down their weapons and surrendered to the military. The dispute served to bring Aboriginal land claims issues to the public's attention.

1990

Eagle Feather

Elijah Harper rose to national prominence when he began a **filibuster**, a political method of stalling, that ended the Meech Lake Accord. When the Canadian Constitution was passed in 1982, it was signed by all provinces except Quebec. The Meech Lake Accord was an attempt to amend

The Oka Crisis

Eagle Feather

1991

The Royal Commission on Aboriginal Peoples is formed.

1992

The First Nations Summit is established in British Columbia.

1993

Parliament endorses the Nunavut Land Claims Agreement.

the Constitution in order to gain Quebec's support. All 10 provinces had to approve the accord for it to be passed. In Manitoba, Harper sat in his legislature seat holding an eagle feather as he refused to vote in favour of the accord, which required unanimous support in the legislature to pass. He refused to give his approval because the accord was not negotiated with input from Aboriginal Peoples, and it failed to recognize the unique status of Canada's Aboriginal Peoples. By refusing to support the Meech Lake Accord, Harper drew national attention to Aboriginal issues in Canada.

1992

Fair Negotiations

The BC Treaty Commission was formed in 1992 by an agreement between the Government of Canada, the Government of British Columbia, and the First Nations of the province. The commission is responsible for ensuring treaty negotiations between the three groups are carried out fairly and effectively. The commission also has a mandate to provide public information and education on treaties and the treaty-making process. A 1991 report on the status of the relationship between First Nations and the provincial government led to the creation of the commission and a new outline for the treaty process. The new treaty process went into effect in 1993 under the direction of the commission. Under the new process, the commission accepts First Nations' negotiation requests, grants federal and provincial funding to support the negotiation process, and monitors the negotiations as they proceed. About 60 percent of British Columbia's First Nations are currently involved in the new treaty process.

Fair Negotiations

1994

The Canadian and British Columbian governments meet with 42 First Nations to discuss treaty negotiations.

1995

A land dispute in Gustafson Lake, British Columbia, leads to a month-long standoff.

Inherent Right

The Charlottetown Accord was a series of proposed amendments to the Canadian Constitution. After the Meech Lake Accord failed, discussions about a new attempt to amend the Constitution began. Prime Minister Brian Mulroney led the campaign to pass the accord. In August 1992, Mulroney met with representatives from the federal, provincial, and territorial governments in Charlottetown, Prince Edward Island. Members of the Assembly of First Nations, the Native Council of Canada, the Inuit Tapirisat of Canada, and the Métis National Council were also in attendance. The meeting led to an agreement between all of the groups involved. The proposed accord would grant greater powers to provincial governments and Aboriginal groups. In the accord, Aboriginal self-government was recognized as an **inherent** right. The Charlottetown Accord was put to a national referendum on October 26. It was defeated by a vote of 54 percent to 46 percent. Most of Eastern Canada supported the accord, but it was defeated in the West. The greatest opponent of the accord was former Prime Minister Pierre Elliott Trudeau, who called the accord a "mess" and urged people to vote against it. He said the accord stripped the federal government of its power.

Inherent Right

1996
The last federal residential school is closed.

1997
The Supreme Court of Canada rules oral history is admissible in court.

1998
Statistics Canada reports there are nearly 800,000 Aboriginal Canadians.

Royal Commission

In 1996, the Royal Commission on Aboriginal Peoples released its 4,000-page report on the status of relations between the Canadian government and Aboriginal Peoples. The report was the result of almost five years of research that included visiting Aboriginal communities across the country and more than 350 studies on Aboriginal relations. The report called for a complete rebuilding of the relationship between Aboriginal and non-Aboriginal people in Canada and the right to self-governance for Aboriginal groups. In addition to these changes, the report suggested a major increase in government funding for Aboriginal programs in the amount of $1.5 to $2 billion per year for 15 years. This money would address health, education, employment, and housing concerns in Aboriginal communities. The federal government, under

Prime Minister Jean Chrétien, responded to the report in January 1998, with a Statement of Reconciliation, which made a formal apology for past injustices toward Aboriginal Peoples. The government promised to renew its relationship with Aboriginal communities and strengthen Aboriginal governance. The government also committed $350 million to support social services programs in Aboriginal communities.

Royal Commission

Into the Future

The Royal Commission on Aboriginal Peoples published a report with recommendations calling for changes in the way Aboriginal Peoples are treated in Canada. Have you observed any instances where Aboriginal Peoples are treated unfairly? How can you contribute to improving the way Aboriginal Peoples are treated in Canada?

1999

Mi'kmaq fishing rights are clarified by the Supreme Court of Canada.

2000

Former Grand Chief of the Northern Quebec Cree, Matthew Coon Come, becomes leader of the Assembly of First Nations.

1982

Charter of Rights and Freedoms

The Charter of Rights and Freedoms is a bill within the Constitution Act. This bill was signed and became law on April 17, 1982. The Charter is a document that guarantees certain political rights to Canadian citizens and civil rights to all Canadians. This includes policies and actions of all levels of government. In the Charter, Aboriginal Peoples were recognized to include First Nations, Inuit, and Métis. The Charter also protected Aboriginal rights or freedoms that had been established by the Royal Proclamation of October 7, 1763, and any rights or freedoms that existed by way of land claims agreements. The Royal Proclamation was

Charter of Rights and Freedoms

CANADIAN CHARTER OF RIGHTS AND FREEDOMS

1981
Aboriginal Peoples petition for the recognition of Aboriginal rights in the Constitution.

1982
The Assembly of First Nations is formed to protect Aboriginal rights.

1983
Aboriginal self-governance is discussed at the First Ministers conference.

created to stabilize relations with Aboriginal Peoples and to regulate trade and land purchases on the western frontier.

1983

Equal Rights

Since 1950, First Ministers conferences have been held annually. A First Ministers conference is a yearly meeting held in Ottawa between the prime minister and provincial premiers and territorial leaders. Each conference has a specific topic for discussion. On March 15 and 16, 1983, the theme of the First Ministers conference was Aboriginal constitutional matters. Some topics discussed during the conference were the Charter of Rights and Freedoms and Aboriginal self-government. For Aboriginal Peoples, self-government involves agreements to govern internal affairs and assume greater responsibility and control over the decisions that impact their communities. This historical meeting, presided over by Prime Minister Trudeau, produced constitutional amendments, such as guaranteeing Aboriginal men and women are entitled to the same rights as other Canadians.

Equal Rights

1984

The Supreme Court rules in favour of the Musqueam First Nation's claim against the British Columbia government.

1985

Under the Constitution Act of Canada, the federal government legislates the Indian Act.

The Indian Act Revised

In 1958, the federal government, on behalf of the Musqueam Indian Band, leased prime land to the Shaughnessy Heights Golf Club in Vancouver for a golf course and club. However, the complete terms of the deal were never revealed to the Aboriginal group. Despite repeated efforts to obtain the document, the group was not provided with a copy of the lease until 1970. The group then discovered the deal had been changed to reduce the amount of rent the Musqueam were paid for the use of their land. In 1975, Chief Delbert Guerin and the Band Council began the process of suing the government. In November 1984, the Supreme Court of Canada awarded the Musqueam people $10 million in compensation.

The Indian Act Revised

1986

The United Church of Canada apologizes for the poor treatment of students at residential schools.

1987

"Iqaluit" becomes the official name of Frobisher Bay.

1988

Ethel Blondin becomes the first Aboriginal woman to serve in the House of Commons.

1985

Restricted Rights and Freedoms

Under the Constitution Act of Canada, the federal government legislated the Indian Act in 1876. Through this act, Aboriginal Peoples were subjected to many restrictions. For example, treaty status was taken away from Métis, Aboriginal Peoples not living on reserves, and Aboriginal women who married non-Aboriginal men. In 1985, Bill C-31, an Act to Amend the Indian Act, was passed. This returned treaty status to many individuals. It eliminated the concept of **enfranchisement,** which meant an Aboriginal person could only obtain certain rights by giving up their treaty status.

Into the Future

The United Nations established The Working Group on Indigenous Populations (WGIP) to promote and protect human rights for indigenous peoples. If you were to start an organization designed to promote and protect a group of people, how would you start? What sort of things could you do as part of the group? What kind of challenges might you face?

1989

The Premier's Council on Native Affairs is created to meet with First Nations and prepare recommendations to the government on a range of issues.

1990

Elijah Harper refuses to give his approval to the Meech Lake Accord.

17

Aboriginal Treaties
1970s

The Red Paper

Citizens Plus, commonly called the *Red Paper*, was the Aboriginal response to the 1969 federal government **white paper** on Aboriginals in Canada. The white paper called for the assimilation of Aboriginal Peoples into mainstream Canadian society. Minister of Indian Affairs, and future prime minister, Jean Chrétien, drafted the white paper, which proposed removing existing laws about Aboriginal Peoples' special status in Canada and their land claims. The white paper gained the support of Prime Minister Trudeau, who believed land claim negotiations should only be carried out between **sovereign** nations. Cree leader Harold Cardinal led the Aboriginal response to the white paper. Cardinal's first response was a book called *The Unjust Society* in 1969. In the book, Cardinal drew attention to inconsistencies between Trudeau's policies and his "just society" platform. In 1970, Cardinal wrote the *Red Paper* to counter each of the points made in the white paper. In 1973, the Supreme Court of Canada ruled that Aboriginal land titles are valid under the law. After, the federal government withdrew the 1969 white paper.

The Red Paper

1971

The **Inuit Tapiriit Kanatami** is founded.

1972

The Indian Control of Indian Education policy is written.

1973

The first Aboriginal reserve in the Northwest Territories is created.

Calder Elected

1972

Calder Elected

In 1972, Frank Calder became the first Aboriginal cabinet minister in Canadian history. This was just one in a long list of firsts for Calder. In 1949, he became the first member of a First Nation to be elected to legislature in Canada. He was also the first Aboriginal to graduate from the Anglican Theological College of the University of British Columbia three years earlier. Calder served in the British Columbia legislature for 26 years. He was a member of the Nisga'a First Nation of northwestern British Columbia. However, Calder is best-known for his landmark court case regarding Aboriginal land titles. In the "Calder vs. Attorney General of British Columbia" case of 1973, Calder argued that Aboriginal claims to traditional lands are valid under the law. The Supreme Court of Canada ruled in favour of recognizing Aboriginal land claims. This would be an important ruling in many land claim cases to follow, including the Nisga'a treaty of May 11, 2000. The Supreme Court's decision also forced the federal government, under Prime Minister Trudeau, to reconsider its Aboriginal policy.

1974

The Native Women's Association of Canada is formed.

1975

Educational Needs of Native Peoples hears requests from Aboriginal Peoples asking for better funding for Aboriginal control of education.

Claim Battles

The Nisga'a Nation of British Columbia fought for more than 100 years before finally reaching a land claims agreement with the federal and provincial governments. The first Nisga'a Land Claims Committee formed in 1890 with the goal of signing a treaty with the Canadian government in regard to Nisga'a land in northwestern British Columbia. However, the federal government did not agree to formally enter into land claims negotiations with the Nisga'a until 1976. The government agreed to the negotiations after a landmark decision by the Supreme Court of Canada in 1973 declared First Nations had legal claim to their traditional lands. The Nisga'a treaty came into effect in 2000. The terms of the treaty protect Nisga'a land and natural resources while forming the outline for Nisga'a self-governance. The Nisga'a treaty was the first modern-day treaty in British Columbia. Since 1976, 14 Aboriginal land claims treaties have been successfully negotiated between First Nations and the federal and provincial governments.

Claim Battles

1976
The Federal government agrees to negotiate with the Nisga'a.

1977
The Berger Commission issues its report.

1978
The Union of British Columbia Indian Chiefs publishes its *Aboriginal Title and Rights Position Paper*.

1977

The Berger Commission

In the early 1970s, many oil companies became interested in building a pipeline through the northern Yukon and Mackenzie River Valley. In 1974, The Mackenzie Valley Pipeline Inquiry was formed to investigate the social, economic, and environmental impact of the proposal. The inquiry was headed by Justice of the Supreme Court of British Columbia Thomas Berger, which led to its more common name, the Berger Commission. Aboriginal Peoples in the region were opposed to the development because of environmental concerns and its infringement of land claims. The Berger Commission was widely covered in the media and brought issues of Aboriginal Peoples and respect for the environment into public view. From 1975 to 1976, the commission members travelled to communities that would be affected by the pipeline.

They held public meetings to discuss the issues surrounding the proposal. In 1977, the Berger report, entitled *Northern Frontier, Northern Homeland* was published. In agreement with the commission's findings, the pipeline was not built.

Into the Future

The term 'First Nation' began to take prominence in the 1970s. Although First Nation does not have a legal definition, the term is used to indicate all the indigenous peoples of Canada. First Nation can also replace the word band in a community. How many First Nations do you know of? How many can you name?

1979

In Canada, 15 residential schools still operate.

1980

Kateri Tekakwitha, a Mohawk woman who died in 1689, is the first North American Aboriginal to be beatified by the Roman Catholic Church.

1960s

White Paper

White Paper

In 1969, Minister of Indian Affairs Jean Chrétien, under the leadership of Pierre Trudeau, presented *The White Paper on Indian Policy*. It proposed complete indigenous assimilation. It also recommended the cancellation of treaty rights, including all of the Crown's policies and commitments made toward indigenous people since the 1763 Royal Proclamation. Prime Minister Trudeau felt this was a way to a "just society," in which all Canadians were equal. Almost unanimously, First Nations agreed the white paper was a means to destroy their culture and history. The 1969 white paper was later withdrawn.

1960s

Gladstone

In 1958, Prime Minister John Diefenbaker named James Gladstone, a member of Alberta's Blood tribe, as the first Aboriginal Senator. His appointment as senator allowed Gladstone to work on positive changes for Aboriginal Peoples in Canada. Gladstone pushed for the enfranchisement of Aboriginal Peoples, though it would be two years before this came into effect. Gladstone retired from the Senate in 1971.

1961

The British Columbia government transfers 24,000 acres of land to the federal government to meet its obligations under Treaty 8.

1962

The North American Indian Brotherhood calls for a legislated Indian claims commission.

1960

Right to Vote

In 1960, John Diefenbaker gave non-enfranchised Aboriginals the right to vote in federal elections. This decision came following a meeting in the House of Commons, when an almost unanimous vote gave Aboriginal Peoples the right to vote without the need to give up treaty rights in exchange. "I felt it was so unjust that they didn't have the vote," Diefenbaker said. By comparison, Aboriginal Peoples in the United States were given the right to vote in the 1920s. Diefenbaker served as Canada's prime minister from 1957 to 1963.

Gladstone

Right to vote

1963

Bill C-130, an Act to Provide for the Disposition of Indian Claims, is introduced in Parliament.

1964

The minister in charge of Indian Affairs commissions the Hawthorn Report to review the situation of Aboriginal Peoples in Canada.

1965

Regina vs. White and Bob clarifies treaty and hunting rights.

1965

Regina vs. White and Bob

Clifford White and David Bob Senior were found in the possession of deer carcasses in Nanaimo, British Columbia. As a result, White and Bob were arrested and charged with hunting out of season under the Game Act. Their case was known as Regina vs. White and Bob. The Supreme Court of Canada ruled that Aboriginal hunting rights protected in the Nanaimo Treaty of 1854 were against provincial laws. Federal Indian Affairs minister Arthur Laing was willing to open treaty negotiations in British Columbia, and asked for a group that represented at least 75 percent of Aboriginals in the province to conduct negotiations. First Nations' attempts to form a province-wide organization failed after Nisga'a Tribal Council decide to proceed on their own with the court case.

Regina vs. White and Bob

1966

The Department of Indian Affairs and Northern Development (DIAND) is formed.

1967

The federal government spends $530 per a year for each Treaty Indian, while it spends $740 a year on the average non-Aboriginal Canadian.

Indian and Eskimo Association

Indian and Eskimo Association

In 1968, leaders of several Aboriginal organizations met with representatives of the Indian and Eskimo Association (IEA). The IEA participated in fundraising and organizing workshops to discuss community and economic development. The workshops also provided support for Aboriginal organizations with regard to government issues. In the meeting, both parties, organization representatives and the IEA agreed that the organizations needed the IEA's support. However, it was decided that the organizations would begin to deal directly with governments, without the IEA acting as a mediator. In 1972, many of the recommendations made during the meeting in 1968 had come into effect. The IEA's name changed to the Canadian Association in Support of Native Peoples to reflect the new functions of the association more accurately.

Into the Future

Before 1960, if an Aboriginal person wanted the right to vote in Canada and to become a full Canadian citizen, he or she had to surrender Indian Status. This was termed enfranchisement. In 1960, Prime Minister John Diefenbaker granted non-enfranchised Aboriginals the right to vote in federal elections. What do you think it would be like not to have the right to vote?

1968
Len Marchand is the first Aboriginal elected to Parliament.

1969
The Department of Indian Affairs takes over control of residential schools.

1970
Indian and Northern Affairs Canada starts transferring local administration of membership to bands.

Aboriginal Treaties
1950s

Changes Made to the Indian Act

1951

Changes Made to the Indian Act

In 1951, Parliament passed the Indian Act. The act contains the primary laws concerning Aboriginal status, governance, reserve land, and communal money. The 1951 Indian Act replaced the previous act of 1876. The revised Indian Act of 1951 removed many of the laws that banned Aboriginal cultural ceremonies. It also added new laws that allowed Aboriginal Peoples to take the government to court over land claims issues. The purpose of these changes was to correct many parts of the 1876 act that were considered unjust. The original Indian Act was based on the idea of assimilating Aboriginal Peoples into Canadian society. The act called for all Aboriginal Peoples to accept enfranchisement. This would give Aboriginal Peoples the right to vote but would cost them their status and culture. The 1876 act went through several revisions in the years after it was first enacted. However, most of these amendments were aimed at promoting assimilation. Aboriginal cultural practices such as the Sun Dance, potlatch, and pow wow were officially banned. The 1951 amendment was the first attempt to remove these laws and grant equal rights to Canadian Aboriginal Peoples.

1951
Parliament amends the Indian Act, removing several unjust laws.

1952
Elsie Knott is the first woman elected chief of her nation.

1953
Inuit families from northern Quebec are relocated to the Arctic.

First Woman Elected Chief

1952

First Woman Elected Chief

When Elsie Knott ran for chief in the 1952 Mud Lake Indian Band election, she had no idea she was about to make history. The band, which is now known as the Curve Lake First Nation, elected Knott the first woman chief in Canada. The federal government had removed laws that prevented women from officially representing Aboriginal Peoples in government one year earlier. Chief Knott went on to become a successful and influential leader. She won the next seven band elections. In total, she served as chief for 16 years, from 1952 to 1962, and again from 1970 to 1976. Knott lost the 1976 election by just 12 votes. As chief, Knott was mostly concerned with improving education on her southern Ontario reserve and helping Aboriginal Peoples gain greater control over their own governance. Growing up on the Ojibwa reserve, Knott only received a grade 8 education. There was no high school on her reserve. She used her role as chief to give children access to better education than she had received.

1956

Aboriginal Peoples Get the Vote

March 10, 1960, was an historic day for Canada's Aboriginal Peoples. That was the day they were granted the right to vote in government elections. Until this day, Aboriginal Peoples in Canada had to give up their status and treaty rights in order to vote in an election. This would have included releasing all claims to land and resources. Due to this, few Aboriginals made this trade to gain voting rights. The motion to grant Aboriginal Peoples the right to vote started in the federal government in 1948. However, it was not until Prime Minister John Diefenbaker pushed it through Parliament that it finally became law.

1954

Parliament promises social and medical services for Newfoundland's Aboriginal communities.

1955

Harry Bertram Hawthorn publishes *The Indians of BC: A Survey of Social and Economic Conditions.*

1958

The First Aboriginal in the Senate

James Gladstone of Kainai First Nation became the first Aboriginal appointed to the Senate on February 1, 1958. This was a full two years before Prime Minister John Diefenbaker granted Aboriginal Peoples the right to vote. Gladstone, or Akay-na-muka, which means

"Many Guns," was a well-known Aboriginal leader for many years before his appointment to Senate. He served as president of the Indian Association of Alberta (IAA) from 1950 to 1953 and again from 1956 to 1957. Gladstone's primary concern as president of the IAA was to **lobby** the federal government to remove unjust laws from the Indian Act. He travelled to Ottawa three times to speak before government on this issue.

Prime Minister Diefenbaker was impressed by Gladstone's work on behalf of Aboriginal rights. Gladstone was sworn in to the Senate on May 12. In his first speech in the Senate, Gladstone spoke in the Blackfoot language "to place in the official debates a few words in the language of my people." Gladstone served in the Senate until March 1971. He died six months later at the age of 84.

The First Aboriginal in the Senate

1956

The Citizenship Act is amended to include Aboriginal Peoples.

1957

The Distant Early Warning line goes into operation in the Arctic.

1958

Chief Mungo Martin presents a **totem pole** to Queen Elizabeth II.

1959

The Battle for Self Governance

The Iroquois are a confederation of six First Nations. This group includes the Mohawk, Oneida, Onondaga, Cayuga, Seneca, and Tuscarora nations. The Iroquois call themselves the Haudenosaunee, or "People of the Longhouse." Since the 1200s, the Iroquois have been governed by a council consisting of the chiefs of all six member nations. This council is known as the Six Nations Confederacy Council. From 1864 until 1924, the council conducted its business in its Council House in Ohsweken, Ontario. In 1924, the Government of Canada seized the Council House and barred the chiefs from entering. The government wanted to prevent Iroquois from maintaining traditional forms of self-governance. The federal government forced the Iroquois to adopt a municipal government of elected members. This is the system of local government used across Canada. When the council of chiefs attempted to take back its building of government in 1959, the RCMP stepped in and locked council members out. On January 1, 2007, the Iroquois chiefs were finally allowed to reclaim their Council House.

The Battle for Self Governance

Into the Future

In 1951, the Indian Act was revised, and many unjust laws were withdrawn. Aboriginal Peoples were given the power to sue the government over land claims. Do you practise a religion or a cultural ceremony at home? Discuss how you would feel if your ceremonies were banned. Why do you think the government felt such ceremonies should be stopped? What would be an effective method for dealing with a ban?

1959

The Nelson Commission publishes its report on Treaties 8 and 11.

1960

Prime Minister Diefenbaker gives Aboriginal Peoples the right to vote in federal elections.

1940s

Indian Act Reform

In the 1940s, a number of Aboriginal leaders pushed the Canadian government for improved rights. Groups emerged to rally public support for the cause. One such group was the League of Indians of Alberta (LIA). In 1946, Parliament created a committee to revise the Indian Act and consulted with groups, including the LIA. The Indian Act was revised in 1951, but it still contained status and enfranchisement clauses.

Indian Act Reform

1940s

Military Involvement

The federal government ruled that it was not mandatory for Aboriginal Peoples to participate in World War II. However, many still volunteered service. More than 4,000 Aboriginal men enlisted to serve in World War II. Aboriginal groups also assisted Canada's war effort in other ways. By the time the war ended, Canadian First Nations donated more than $23,000 toward the war effort. Many First Nations sent additional donations directly to the British War Victims Fund, Red Cross, and other charities.

1943

World War

In 1943, the Canadian government ruled all able-bodied Aboriginal men of military age could be called on to represent Canada in wars overseas. This went against existing treaty negotiations, which stated Aboriginal Peoples would not be involved in battles involving Great Britain. In response to the government ruling, many Aboriginal groups protested with marches. These groups also signed petitions that were delivered to the federal government in Ottawa. The issue of Aboriginal participation in wars was discussed in the House of Commons. In 1944, the war cabinet committee decided to no longer make it mandatory for Aboriginal Peoples to represent Canada in overseas wars.

Military Involvement

1941

The Crerar-Gray agreement is made, creating measures for dealing with **cut-off lands**.

1942

Aboriginal commercial fishermen are required to pay federal income tax.

World War

1943	1944	1945
More than 4,000 Canadian Aboriginals volunteer as soldiers in World War II.	The Federation of Saskatchewan Indians forms.	The Second World War ends.

1948

United Nations

Canada signed the United Nations Universal Declaration of Human Rights in December 1948. This bill, which has been described as the most translated document in the world, was the first worldwide statement of the rights humans are entitled. The declaration resulted in Canada's government re-examining its treatment of Aboriginals for the first time. Many Aboriginal Peoples saw this as a major opportunity for improved rights in Canada.

1949

Newfoundland and Labrador

When Newfoundland and Labrador entered **Confederation** with Canada in 1949, the province's Aboriginal Peoples were not included in the process. The governments of Canada and Newfoundland decided against including Aboriginal Peoples in the Terms of Union. When the National Convention of Newfoundland met to discuss Confederation, delegates suggested that the Canadian government accept responsibility for all of Canada's people. This included its Aboriginal population. However, the Canadian government did not follow this suggestion. The National Convention included 45 elected members. Its function was to review the Newfoundland's economic changes.

United Nations

1946

Peter Kelly and Andrew Paull press for revisions to the Indian Act.

1947

First Nations people are given the right to vote in provincial elections.

1948

The United Nations enacts the Universal Declaration of Human Rights.

Into the Future

The United Nations Universal Declaration of Human Rights is based on the 'Four Freedoms' the U.S. government adopted during the Second World War. This includes freedom of speech, freedom of conscience, freedom from fear, and freedom from want. Can you name more freedoms that you think are important? Can you name some other basic human rights you feel all people, regardless of race, are entitled to?

1949
Nisga'a Chief Frank Calder is elected to the British Columbia Legislature.

1950
The Indian Claims Commission is created.

33

1930s

Land and Natural Resources Acts

1930

Land and Natural Resources Acts

When the provinces of Manitoba, Saskatchewan, and Alberta joined Confederation, the federal government took control of all land and natural resources. Other provinces had retained control over their land and resources when they joined Canada. The federal government argued that retaining control of prairie land was necessary in order to aid programs to promote settlement in Western Canada. However, many people in the Prairie Provinces thought these laws were unfair. In 1930, the federal government signed Natural Resources Transfer Acts with each of the three Prairie Provinces. Under these acts, each province gained control over all Crown lands and natural resources within its borders. The acts also included a number of clauses designed to protect Aboriginal and treaty rights. This included hunting and fishing rights and the right to select reserve land. However, many Aboriginal groups felt they should have been included in the process of negotiating these laws.

1931

The Native Brotherhood of British Columbia is formed.

1932

The Métis Association of Alberta is formed.

1933

The Alberta government agrees to research Métis concerns.

Mural Debate

In 1932, British Columbia Provincial Secretary S.L. Howe commissioned a series of murals from B.C. artist George Southwell. Howe wanted the murals to represent courage, labour, enterprise, and justice. He thought these were important concepts in the province's history. By 1935, Southwell had finished painting the murals in the B.C. legislature building. The murals were meant to show historic scenes from the province's past. However, many people felt the paintings depicted Canadian Aboriginal Peoples in a negative way. One mural showed Aboriginal women carrying baskets of salmon and large logs under the direction of European men. In 2001, a formal report to the legislature recommended removing the murals. The debate continued for another six years. Some members of the legislative assembly argued that removing the murals would be the same as removing a piece of history. Others said the murals were offensive to many people who should feel welcomed in a government building. These people recommended moving the murals to an art gallery or museum. However, this plan was put on hold when the cost of moving the murals without damaging either the paintings or the legislature building was estimated to cost as much as $1 million. In 2007, the provincial government voted in favour of hiding the murals from view behind a false wall.

Mural Debate

1934

The Ewing Commission is formed to investigate Métis concerns in the province of Alberta.

1935

The Prairie Farm Rehabilitation Act creates community pastures and later forces the removal of Métis living along unused Crown land.

United Alberta's First Nations

1936

The position of Superintendent-General of Indian Affairs is abolished. The minister of mines assumes responsibility for Aboriginal issues.

1937

The Fraser Salmon Convention is signed by Canada and the U.S.

United Alberta's First Nations

Although the Indian Act did not allow Aboriginal Canadians to form political organizations, the Cree and Stoney First Nations of central Alberta united to form the League of Indians of Alberta (LIA) in 1933. John Callihoo became president of the LIA in 1937. Callihoo's work on behalf of Aboriginal rights earned him the nickname "The Lawyer" from members of the Department of Indian Affairs. In 1939, Callihoo reorganized the LIA into the Indian Association of Alberta (IAA). The association grew in size and influence in the following years. By the 1940s, the IAA had united most of the First Nations in Alberta. In 1946, southern Alberta Blood First Nations formed local IAA chapters. James Gladstone, who worked to unite the Blood and Cree Nations, was named IAA director the same year. The IAA became active in lobbying the provincial and federal governments for Aboriginal concerns. The IAA was later involved in planning legislative changes to the 1951 Indian Act amendment.

Into the Future

In 1937, the Dene in the Northwest Territories refused treaty payments from the government as a means of protesting the loss of their rights and control. It was a peaceful but powerful means of protest. What are some other peaceful ways to protest bias?

1938

The Métis Population Betterment Act is passed, allowing Métis to set land aside for reserves.

1939

Canada joins World War II.

1940

The Ogdensburg Agreement places military defences in the Arctic.

Aboriginal Treaties
1920s

Frederick Ogilvie Loft

Frederick Ogilvie Loft

Frederick Ogilvie Loft, known as F. O. Loft, was a Aboriginal rights activist, veteran of World War I, and member of the Mohawk Nation. He formed the League of Indians of Canada in Ontario. Loft argued for the rights of the indigenous peoples of Canada. He tried to bring to an end to the restrictions on hunting on Aboriginal lands, policies of assimilation that would destroy Aboriginal culture, and poor living conditions on reserves.

1920

Assimilation

In 1920, an amendment to the Indian Act changed the lives of Aboriginal children living in Canada. The amendment made it mandatory for Aboriginal children to attend residential schools. These schools were created to force Aboriginal Peoples into assimilating with European ways of life. Often kidnapped, Aboriginal children were sent to government-funded schools at churches of various denominations. At the residential schools, Aboriginal children were forced to practise **Christianity**. These children were also punished for speaking their own language or practising their own faith. Allegations of abuse were also connected to residential schools.

1920s

The Williams Treaties

In the late 1700s, many treaties were created informally. In some cases, Aboriginal Peoples were given nothing more than a blank document to sign. The purpose of the Williams Treaties was to address outstanding Aboriginal land claims in southern and central Ontario. The land in question spanned about 28,000 square kilometres. The Williams Treaties were the last of the historical Indian treaties in Canada. These treaties were named after the federal government's chief negotiator, Angus Williams. They were signed by seven Chippewa and Mississauga First Nations of Southern Ontario and members of the Government of Canada. Different from treaties signed prior to the Williams Treaties, hunting and fishing rights were not secured for Aboriginals of the area.

Assimilation

1921
Several Aboriginal groups give land rights to the Mackenzie River area to the federal government.

1922
The federal government removes some salmon fishing restrictions from Aboriginal Peoples.

1923
Aboriginal boarding schools become residential schools.

The Williams Treaties

1924

The Six Nations Confederacy Council is locked out of their traditional government building by the federal government.

1925

Powwows, sweat lodges and Sun Dances are banned.

Treaty 11

Prior to 1920, the Canadian government had little interest in treaty talks in northwestern British Columbia. This was because the land in this area was not considered well-suited for farming practices. However, this changed when oil was discovered in the Mackenzie Valley. Government officials considered the potential for development, including large-scale oil exploration in the area, and sent treaty commissioners to the area to begin negotiations on what became known as Treaty 11. Approximately 620,000 square kilometres of land was addressed in Treaty 11. In addition to a monetary payment, the treaty involved the Canadian government providing medals, flags, clothing, hunting and fishing equipment, and agricultural tools. When oil exploration did not result in a profit for government officials, non-Aboriginal activity in the Mackenzie Valley area soon decreased. Treaty 11 was the last of the numbered treaties.

Treaty 11

1926

Chief William Pierrish of Neskonlith represents British Columbia First Nations in a formal petition to the king of Great Britain.

1927

The Indian Act prohibits Aboriginal Peoples from raising money or hiring lawyers to pursue land claims.

1924

Ohsweken

The Council House in Ohsweken was built in 1864 and was important to traditional leaders on the Akwesasne reserve. The Council House served as the home to the Six Nations Confederacy Council. When the Council House was seized by the Royal Canadian Mountain Police (RCMP) on October 7, 1924, documents and wampum belts that proved the sovereignty

Ohsweken

of the traditional government were seized. The people of Ohsweken were forced to stop their traditional system of governance, which involved a council of chiefs. An elected band council was implemented in its place. This meant council positions were awarded through an election.

1927

Allied Tribes

Members of the Allied Tribes of British Columbia (ATBC) travelled to Ottawa for a meeting to discuss Aboriginal rights and land title claims. Following the meeting with a committee of Senate and House of Commons members, claims by the ATBC were dismissed.

Allied Tribes

The committee argued that the ATBC did not prove their rights and land claims during the talks. The committee then recommended the barring of future land claims. Following the meeting, Parliament amended the Indian Act so that collecting funds for the purpose of advancing claims, would be illegal.

Into the Future

Between 1871 and 1921, the Crown made Treaties 1-11, also known as the numbered treaties, with indigenous peoples for the purposes of agriculture, settlement, and the use of natural resources. Another term for the numbered treaties was the Land **Cessation** Treaties. First Nations gave up large portions of land in exchange for money, reserves of land, and education for their children. If you were in this position, what terms would you agree to in exchange for your land? Discuss possible trade goods or services that are important to you. What sort of responsibilities would you hold your trade partner to?

1928

A federal government official predicts all Aboriginal students in residential schools will be assimilated within two decades.

1929

Approximately 80 residential schools exist across Canada, the most ever at any one time.

Aboriginal Health in Decline

1913

Aboriginal Health in Decline

Between 1904 and 1913, the state of health for most Canadian Aboriginal Peoples was declining. In 1907, Canada's chief medical officer for the Department of the Interior and Indian Affairs, Dr. P.H. Bryce, published a report on residential schools in Manitoba and the Northwest Territories. In the report, Bryce stated that Aboriginal health care was in need of major upgrading. He reported that between 1883 and 1907, 24 percent of Aboriginal children in these schools died either while still in school or shortly after leaving. The most common cause of death was tuberculosis, which had a death rate 20 times higher among Aboriginal Peoples than

Canadians of European descent. Dr. Bryce also predicted that, if the trend continued, Canada's Aboriginal population would drop by nearly 2,000 in the following six years. This was in contrast to a population increase of 20,000, which Dr. Bryce said would have been natural in the same time period. Minister of the Interior and Superintendent General of Indian Affairs Clifford Sifton later acknowledged the declining state of Aboriginal health care. However, it was not until 1979 and the signing of the Indian Health Transfer Policy that Canadian Aboriginal Peoples gained control over their own health care.

1914

The Dollar Replaces the Made Beaver

The fur trade played a major role in Canada's early history between European settlers and Aboriginal Peoples. By 1914, Canada's cash economy had extended to the fur trade and the Hudson's Bay Company (HBC). HBC started establishing fur trading posts in Canada in 1670, and it was not long before the company thought it necessary to create a standard unit of currency. The issue they faced was combining the Aboriginal **bartering system** with European bookkeeping practices. The company decided to create the "Made Beaver" as its standard of trade. A Made Beaver

1910

Aboriginal groups protest the breaking of a treaty promise at Parliament Hill in Ottawa.

1912

The Quebec Boundaries Extensions Act pushes Quebec's boundaries into land populated by Aboriginal Peoples.

The Dollar Replaces the Made Beaver

was a top-quality beaver pelt that was already stretched, tanned, and ready for trade. HBC then set all of its prices in relation to the Made Beaver. In 1733, HBC charged 10 Made Beavers for a rifle or four for a pistol. A hatchet cost half a Made Beaver. Over time, the company started using copper tokens marked with a number followed by the letters MB. A token marked "5MB" was worth five Made Beavers. These tokens were mainly replaced by cash in 1914. However, the tokens remained in use in remote regions of the Arctic as late as 1955.

1918

Migratory Bird Treaty Act

In 1918, the United States and Canada agreed to the Migratory Bird Treaty Act. This act sought to protect migratory birds by making it illegal to hunt, capture, buy, or sell migratory birds. This law also included bird parts, such as feathers. Many Aboriginal Peoples protested the act because of the significance of bird feathers in many First Nations spiritual beliefs. The act was later amended to allow Aboriginal Peoples to obtain eagle feathers and other parts of migratory birds that are important to their spirituality.

Migratory Bird Treaty Act

1915

The Allied Tribes of British Columbia forms to work toward land claims and treaties.

1916

The McKenna-McBride Commission publishes its final report on British Columbia's First Nations reserves.

Aboriginal Treaties
1900s

Treaty Nine

1905

Treaty Nine

From 1899 to 1921, Treaties Eight to Eleven were signed by Canada's Aboriginal Peoples. Treaty Nine was signed in 1906, and addressed lands in northern Ontario. Another name for Treaty Nine is the James Bay Treaty. This is because the eastern end of the territory in the treaty is the James Bay, which is a large body of water on the southern end of Hudson Bay. Canada's two federal commissioners, Samuel Stewart and Duncan Campbell Scott, along with Ontario commissioner Daniel McMartin, were appointed to negotiate the treaty. The treaty negotiations involved offering Aboriginal Peoples money, reserves, and the construction of schools. Aboriginals were also provided with the opportunity to hunt and fish on the land, as they had done before. Treaty Nine was negotiated and created during the summers of 1905 and 1906.

1901

St. George's Residential School is established in Lytton, British Columbia.

1902

The *Dominion of Canada Schedule of All Indian Reserves* is published.

1903

The Songhees people are displaced from their Victoria-area reserve by a special act of Parliament.

Treaty Ten

Chief Joe Capilano

Treaty Ten

Treaty Ten was negotiated by Treaty Commissioner J.A.J. McKenna, who was also responsible for the negotiation of Treaty Eight. During the negotiation, McKenna agreed to provide aid in education and medical services, reserve lands, money, clothing, and hunting and fishing rights. The main concern for the First Nations involved, however, was that they could retain their traditional way of life. McKenna agreed that Aboriginal Peoples would continue to earn a livelihood in the same way after the treaty was signed as they had before. The section of land addressed in Treaty Ten spanned 220,000 square kilometres in Alberta and Saskatchewan.

1900s

Chief Joe Capilano

Squamish Chief Joe Capilano was an Aboriginal rights activist. With other Aboriginal leaders, he travelled to Ottawa, and then London, England, to talk about Aboriginal rights. In London, he met with King Edward VII and Queen Alexandra and lobbied for the need to recognize Aboriginal land claims. Many areas in British Columbia have been named after Chief Joe Capilano as a tribute to his activism. These areas include Capilano Lake and Capilano River.

1904

Aboriginal Peoples from British Columbia participate in St. Louis World Fair.

1905

The province of Alberta is formed.

ACTIVITY
Make a Treaty

Aboriginal Peoples agreed to share their ancestral lands in exchange for money and promises of certain rights from settlers. Each group learned something from the others' traditions and found ways to co-exist. Treaties brought different groups of people together. The ideal goal of a treaty is to create a peaceful and fair exchange and agreement.

Write a Treaty

To learn more about how treaties affect groups of people, participate in an activity with another class at your school. One classroom should take on the role of European settlers, and the other should take on the role of Aboriginal Peoples. As the settler class, discuss the challenges and benefits of moving to the other classroom. As a class, decide what you are prepared to offer as payment for moving in. Choose representatives from each class to negotiate the terms of the deal. Both classes must decide on rules that the other class must follow. The class will be crowded, so there must be boundaries of where the "settlers" are allowed to sit and move in the space. Both classes must find a way to have their regular lessons of the day. This will involve scheduling and promises of mutual respect between groups. Once you have decided on your terms of payment and conduct, draw up a written agreement, or treaty. Everyone in both classes must sign the treaty. The settler class will move in and co-exist with the other class for one day.

After the exercise is over, reflect on the idea of treaties. Did this exercise give you a deeper appreciation and awareness of how treaties have affected the citizens of Canada? Discuss the particular challenges of your group, and share your experiences with all the participants of this exercise.

FURTHER
Research

There are many books and websites that can provide more information about Aboriginal treaties.

Websites

Canada in the Making is a website devoted to understanding how Aboriginal Peoples and European settlers shaped Canada into the country it is today.
www.canadiana.org/citm/index_e.html

Visit Aboriginal Canada Portal to learn more about Canadian Aboriginal Peoples.
www.aboriginalcanada.gc.ca

Glossary

bartering system: traditional Aboriginal system of trading items of equal value

cessation: to bring to a stop or end

Christianity: the main religion of European settlers

Confederation: the joining of independent provinces to form Canada

Crown, the: a term that refers to the highest level of government

cut-off lands: parts of Aboriginal reserve lands taken from them by the government

enfranchisement: process of gaining the right to vote; for Aboriginal Peoples, this meant giving up their status and treaty rights

filibuster: an action by a member of a legislative assembly that stalls the proceedings

First Nation: Canadian Aboriginal Peoples who are not Inuit or Métis

Indian Act: the Government of Canada's primary legislation concerning Aboriginal Peoples and the law

inherent: something that is built-in, a natural part

Inuit: Aboriginal Peoples of Canada's northern region

Inuit Tapiriit: an organization that represents Inuit

Iroquois League: a group of six First Nations under one governmental structure

lobby: attempt to influence the members of a legislature

Métis: people of mixed European and Aboriginal descent

non-confidence: a vote in the legislature in which members vote to end the current government's term and call an election

reserves: land set aside by the federal government for Aboriginal Peoples

sovereign: having complete, independent authority and self-governance

totem pole: a traditional carved tree trunk made by West Coast First Nations

white paper: a government report that addresses a certain issue; used to aid in making decisions on policy but is not itself legislation

Index